The Iron Man

Classroom Questions

A SCENE BY SCENE TEACHING GUIDE

Amy Farrell

SCENE BY SCENE
ENNISKERRY, IRELAND

Copyright © 2017 by Scene by Scene.

Without limiting the rights under copyright, this book is sold subject to the condition that it shall not, by way of trade or otherwise be lent, resold, hired out, reproduced, stored on or introduced into a retrieval system, or transmitted, in any form or by any means (electronic, mechanical, photocopying, recording or otherwise), or otherwise circulated, without the publisher's prior consent, in any form other than that in which it is published and without a similar condition, including this condition, being imposed on the subsequent publisher.

All rights reserved. No part of this publication may be recorded or transmitted in any form or by any means electronic, mechanical, photocopying, recording or otherwise without the proper consent of the publisher.

The publisher reserves the right to change, without notice, at any time, the specification of this product, whether by change of materials, colours, format, text revision or any other characteristic.

Scene by Scene
Enniskerry
Wicklow, Ireland.
www.scenebysceneguides.com

The Iron Man Classroom Questions by Amy Farrell.
ISBN 978-1-910949-64-1

Contents

Chapter One - 'The Coming of the Iron Man' 1

Chapter Two - 'The Return of the Iron Man' 6

Chapter Three - 'What's to be Done with the Iron Man?' 13

Chapter Four - 'The Space-Being and the Iron Man' 18

Chapter Five - 'The Iron Man's Challenge' 23

Further Questions 31

Chapter One
'The Coming of the Iron Man'

Summary

The huge Iron Man stands on the cliff-top, at night. Nobody knows where he comes from or how he was made.

He listens to the sea and searches it with his eyes, having never seen it before.

He steps off the cliff and tumbles, crashing down onto the rocks, breaking into pieces.

Silence follows and the sounds of the sea. Nobody knows the Iron Man has fallen.

As day breaks, a seagull takes one of the Iron Man's eyes back to his mate. The eye looks at them.

A gull retrieves one of the Iron Man's hands. The eye looks at it. The hand picks the eye up. Now it can see.

It jabs each of the gulls in turn and they fly away.

The hand scuttles over the stones, searching, and finds an arm. It also finds the other hand, which joins with it.

Gradually, the hands find body parts and fit the Iron Man back together.

He cannot find one of his ears and searches for it. It is on the gull's nesting ledge.

The Iron Man looks at the sea and walks into it, perhaps looking for his ear.

The gulls circle overhead as he disappears and walks out to sea.

Questions

1. Where is the Iron Man?

2. What are the origins of the Iron Man?

3. Describe the Iron Man.
   Does he sound friendly or menacing to you?
   Give a reason for your answer.

4. How does the Iron Man react to the sea?
   Can you explain this reaction?

5. Describe the Iron Man's eyes.

6. What happens when the Iron Man steps off the cliff?

7. What happens after the Iron Man has fallen?

8. What of the Iron Man's, does the seagull take?

9. What does this object do?
   What is your response to this?

10. What do the gulls think this object is?

11. What "strange crab" do the gulls find?

12. What happens once these objects are together?

13. What does the hand do, once it can see?
    Why, do you think, does it do this?

Should the hand be grateful to the gulls?
Explain your point of view.

14. What does the hand do next?

15. Comment on the image of the sighted hand scampering over the stones.
Is this a pleasant image?
What does it make you think of?

16. What does the hand do when it finds the other hand?

17. What do the hands manage to do?
Are you impressed by their abilities here?
Is there anything funny about this scene, or is it serious?

18. What body part is the Iron Man unable to find?
Where is it?
Is it of use to the gulls?

19. What does the Iron Man do next?
Why does he do this, in your opinion?

20. What happens to the Iron Man's eyes?

21. A "line of bubbles" moves out to sea.
What is causing these bubbles?

22. Do you think the Iron Man is in danger?
Develop your answer fully.

23. Do you think that people know about the Iron Man?
Refer to the story to support your ideas.

24. What, do you think, is the Iron Man's backstory?

25. Is there a lot of nature imagery and description of the natural world in this chapter?
Include examples to support your answer.

26. What illustrations would you include for this chapter if you were the story's illustrator?

27. How does the author make the Iron Man seem mysterious?

28. What questions do you have about this story so far?

Chapter Two
'The Return of the Iron Man'

Summary

Hogarth, a farmer's son, fishes until it gets too dark. He listens to the owls and the sea.

He has the strange feeling of being watched. Feeling afraid, he looks up at the cliff and sees two green lights. The lights rise into the sky as the Iron Man climbs over the cliff-top.

Hogarth runs home and tells his family about the Iron Man.

His father believes him. He takes down his gun and drives to the next farm, but the farmer there just laughs at him.

Hogarth's father drives on to the next farm after that, where he is believed. This farmer suggests investigating the next day.

As Hogarth's father turns his car, his headlights shine on a half eaten tractor, lying there with teethmarks in it.

The men are scared. The farmer runs indoors. Hogarth's father starts driving as fast as he can.

He slows down to look at headlamps in a treetop and a giant foot comes down in the middle of the road. A giant hand reaches for the car. Hogarth's father drives at the foot, crashing into it, toppling the giant Iron Man. Hogarth's father gets home safely.

The next day the farmers are angry because their farm machinery is gone. They find pieces of machinery with giant teethmarks in them.

A trail of giant footsteps leads to each of the farms with missing equipment.

The footsteps lead back to the top of the cliff and marks on the rocks below show where a huge body has slid down.

The farmers shout angrily, wondering what they should do about the Iron Man. They cannot call the police or the Army for help, as nobody will believe them.

They dig a huge hole and cover it with branches, straw and soil, as a trap for the Iron Man. They use an old rusty lorry for bait. When they catch him, they will bury him forever in the hole.

The farmers are excited when they check their trap the next day, but it is undisturbed. They check day after day, but the Iron Man never comes.

The farmers begin to wonder if he will ever come again. They wonder if he ever came at all, and make up other explanations for what happened to their farm machinery.

The owner of the red lorry takes it away.

Although the hole is dangerous, they do not want to fill it in, in case the Iron Man returns. They put up a danger notice to keep people away from it.

The little boy Hogarth decides to use the hole to trap a fox. He throws a dead hen onto the hole's covering and waits for a fox.

A fox arrives, but it circles the hole, not stepping out onto it.

The fox looks towards the cliff-top and sees the Iron Man, before vanishing.

Hogarth climbs down the tree he is in, to go to his father. He stops at the tree's base, unsure of where the Iron Man is.

He realises that the Iron Man is eating the barbed wire fence. Hogarth knows that the fence will not take the Iron Man towards the hole, so he strikes a nail and knife together to get the Iron Man's attention.

The Iron Man follows the metallic sound and falls into the pit.

The farmers are delighted.

The Iron Man's eyes burn different colours and his cogs grind and screech inside him.

The farmers begin to bury the Iron Man while he roars.

Soon he is silent, buried beneath a mound of earth.

The farmers go home, talking cheerfully.

Hogarth feels guilty for luring the Iron Man into the pit.

Questions

1. Why does Hogarth stop fishing?

2. What sounds can Hogarth hear?

3. What strange feeling does he have?
   Describe this feeling.

4. What does Hogarth see at the top of the cliff?

5. What happens, as Hogarth watches?

6. How is the Iron Man described?
   Does he sound menacing or peaceful to you?
   Give reasons for your answer.

7. How does Hogarth respond to this sight?
   What would you do, in his position?

8. How do Hogarth's family respond to news of the Iron Man?

9. How does the farmer at the next farm react to news of the Iron Man?

10. How does the second farmer respond to news of the Iron Man?

What does he suggest they do?
Is this a good strategy, do you think?

11. What does Hogarth's father see as he turns his car in the yard?
What has happened here?
What does this suggest about the Iron Man?

12. The men are puzzled and afraid.
How would you feel, in their position?

13. What is the weather like on this night?
How does this detail add to the atmosphere?

14. What happens when Hogarth's father slows down to look at the headlamps in the treetop?

15. How does Hogarth's father escape?
Was this a clever thing to do, do you think?

16. Why are the farmers angry the next morning?

17. What clue have they discovered?
What second clue do they discover?
What do these clues reveal?

18. How would you feel, if you were one of the farmers?

19. Why do the farmers begin to shout?

20. Why can't they call the police or the Army?

21. What action do they take against the Iron Man?
    Do you think this is a good idea?

22. What do they use as bait?

23. What will they do when they catch the Iron Man?
    What is your response to this plan?
    Do you feel sorry for the Iron Man at all?

24. How are the farmers feeling the next morning?

25. What do the farmers expect to find?

26. What do they find?

27. What do the farmers begin to doubt?

28. What happens to the red lorry?

29. What do they do with the hole?

30. What idea does the little boy Hogarth have?
    Does his plan work?

31. What makes the fox vanish?

32. Why does Hogarth stop at the bottom of the tree?
    What is the Iron Man doing?

33. What frightening idea does Hogarth have?

34. How does the Iron Man react to the sound of metal?

35. Is Hogarth clever to lure the Iron Man into the hole like this?

36. How does the Iron Man react to being in the hole?

37. Why does Hogarth shout as he runs home?

38. What do the farmers do when they see the Iron Man in their pit?
How does the Iron Man react?
How must he be feeling?

39. What do the farmers do, now that they have caught the Iron Man?
How does the Iron Man respond?
How do you feel, reading this section?

40. How does Hogarth feel as the chapter ends?
How would you feel, in his position?

41. Does the Iron Man deserve to be buried alive like this? Give reasons for your answer.

42. What is the mood like as this chapter ends?

43. If you were the illustrator, what drawings would you include in this chapter?

Chapter Three
'What's to be Done with the Iron Man?'

Summary

By spring the following year, the mound over the Iron Man is a grassy hill. People begin to picnic there.

A family stop to have a picnic on the hill. The father feels the ground shake and explains how distant earthquakes can be felt.

The mother gasps. The tablecloth sags in its centre and falls into a crack in the ground. The crack widens and lengthens, dividing the family from each other.

A huge iron hand comes up through the crack. The family run to their car and drive away.

They do not see the Iron Man freeing himself from the pit.

The farmers decide to call the Army, but Hogarth has an idea they agree to try first.

Hogarth and the farmers approach the Iron Man and Hogarth speaks to him. Hogarth offers the Iron Man all the iron and metal he wants to eat, if he will stop eating up the farms. Hogarth apologises for trapping and burying the Iron Man.

The Iron Man follows Hogarth and the farmers through the villages to a great scrap-metal yard.

The Iron Man's eyes turn red and he begins to eat.

Hogarth visits him every few days. The Iron Man is happy, and no longer rusty, eating constantly.

Questions

1. What imagery does the author use to show that time has passed?

2. Describe the hill over the Iron Man.

3. What is the hill used as?

4. What do the family have with them for their picnic? Does this sound appetising to you?

5. What does the father notice?

6. What does he explain to the little boy?

7. Why does the mother yelp?

8. What happens to their tablecloth? Comment on this image.

9. Is this a funny or scary moment, in your opinion?

10. Describe the crack in the ground. Did you expect something like this to happen?

11. What do the family do?

12. What do the family not see?

13. How do the farmers respond to this development?

14. What do they want to do next?

15. What does the newly escaped Iron Man eat?

16. "He really was a monster."
    Why do the farmers feel this way about the Iron Man?
    Is he a monster, in your view?

17. What deal does Hogarth offer the Iron Man?

18. Hogarth apologises to the Iron Man.
    Do you think this is important?
    Why/Why not?

19. How would you feel, in Hogarth's position, talking to this iron giant?

20. Are you surprised that the Iron Man follows Hogarth?

21. How do people react to the sight of the Iron Man marching behind the farmers?
    How would you react, do you think?

22. Where do they bring the Iron Man?
    What does the Iron Man do when he reaches the scrap-metal yard?

23. "Hogarth visited the Iron Man every few days."
    Why does he do this?
    What does this tell you about Hogarth?

24. What change comes over the Iron Man?

25. What is the mood like in this chapter?
    Where does it change?

26. Are you happy with how things with the Iron Man have been resolved?

Chapter Four
'The Space-Being and the Iron Man'

Summary

Everybody is talking about a star in the Constellation of Orion that is getting bigger.

It grows until it is the size of the moon. It is a deep, gloomy red.

It is getting bigger as it gets nearer to the world. It it hits the world at speed, it will blast it to pieces. Everyone is worried.

Then, it seems to stop. The astronomers notice a tiny black speck appear in the middle of the star.

By the fifth night, this speck is seen flying from the giant star's centre towards earth. It is some sort of flying creature.

Each night, this winged horror is bigger. It blots out the red star as it approaches earth.

It lands in Australia. The shock of its landing is felt around the world.

It is a terrific dragon, a terrible creature, covering all of Australia.

Everybody waits and wonders what it has come for.

The next day, it speaks, wanting to be fed living things. If it is not fed as it wishes, it will eat whatever it can and leave the world looking like a charred pebble.

The peoples of the world get together and reason that they could never satisfy this creature's appetite. Rather than feed it, they decide to fight it.

They launch a prolonged attack, using everything they have, including rockets, bombs, and missiles.

The dragon smiles when their attack dies down. This worries the people of the world.

The dragon speaks again. It gives the peoples of the world a week to prepare its first meal, otherwise it will start on the cities and towns.

The peoples of the earth begin to lament. Everybody is talking and worrying about this.

Hogarth goes to the Iron Man for help.

He does not want to help at first, but Hogarth points out that without life on earth, there will be no scrap metal for him.

The Iron Man thinks for a moment. Then he has the idea of going out as the champion of the earth against this monster from space.

Questions

1. What is everybody talking about?

2. How do people feel about this strange news?

3. As it grows, what does this thing look like?
   How would you feel, if you saw such a sight in the night sky?

4. Why is this star getting bigger?

5. What will happen if it hits the world at speed?

6. What strange thing suddenly happens to the star?

7. What "next strange thing" do the astronomers notice?

8. What do the astronomers see on the fifth night?
   Comment on the imagery here.
   How would you feel if you were one of the astronomers observing this?

9. What, do you think, is emerging from the star?

10. "Then, for one awful night, its wings seemed to be filling most of the sky."
    How would people react if something like this happened today, do you think?

11. Where does the winged creature land?

12. What is the effect of its landing?

13. What is this winged creature?

14. Describe the creature.

15. What is it like now for the Australians?

16. What do the people of earth do while the space-bat-angel-dragon lies resting?

17. What does the space-bat-angel-dragon want?

18. What will happen if it does not get what it wants?

19. What do the peoples of the world decide to do?
    Why do they decide on this course of action?
    Does this sound like a good plan to you?

20. Describe the attack on the creature.
    Is it successful?

21. How does the dragon respond to this attack?

22. What message does the space-bat-angel-dragon have when it speaks again?

23. How do the world leaders react to this message?

24. Who does Hogarth go to for help?

25. How does Hogarth convince the Iron Man to help him?

26. What idea does the Iron Man have?
    Is this a good idea, do you think?
    Are you surprised that the Iron Man makes this offer? Why/why not?

27. What illustrations would you include in this chapter?

28. What makes this chapter tense?

29. What is the mood like as this chapter ends?

30. Will the Iron Man be a match for this space creature, in your view?

Chapter Five
'The Iron Man's Challenge'

Summary

The Iron Man is taken to pieces and flown to Australia.

A ship brings iron girders from China and another brings fuel oil from Japan.

A team of engineers fit the Iron Man's parts together, near the space-bat-angel-dragon's neck.

The Iron Man shouts at the dragon to sit up and take notice.

The dragon is surprised and listens to the tiny Iron Man, who challenges it to a test of strength.

The space-bat-angel-dragon laughs at a tiny creature like the Iron Man challenging it to a test like this.

If the Iron Man wins, the dragon must become his slave.

The space-bat-angel-dragon is so astounded that it agrees.

The engineers have fashioned a huge iron bed out of girders, with a steel-lined pit beneath it. The pit is filled with fuel oil and set alight.

The Iron Man lies on this grid, turning red-hot.

The space-bat-angel-dragon watches in astonishment.

When the fuel burns away, the Iron Man stands up. He says if the creature cannot stand to be red-hot like him, then it is weaker than him and is his slave.

The monster laughs and tells the Iron Man to build his fire, knowing that he will not be able to build one big enough.

The Iron Man tells it to go and lie on the sun until it is red-hot.

The creature agrees and flies towards the sun while the world watches.

It lands on the sun, glowing blue, then red, then orange, and finally white.

It returns to earth and lands heavily, charred and blackened.

The Iron Man responds by lying once more on his bed of flames.

The creature watches in horror, knowing that this means it will have to return to the sun's flames.

Although the Iron Man grins as he becomes white hot, he is terribly afraid that if the flames get fiercer, he will melt.

The engineers also fear it could be the end of the Iron Man.

Just as he begins to melt, the fuel is used up and the flames die.

He gets up and points to the sun. The dragon does not laugh, but sets off for the sun. Although the last time was dreadful, it does not want to let the Iron Man win.

He lands on the sun as before. This time he returns very slowly and lands more heavily than ever on Australia. He is exhausted.

His wings are rags and his skin is crisped. His fatness has been changed to precious stones by the sun's heat. They burst through his scorched skin and fall to the desert.

The Iron Man announces round three. The space-bat-angel-dragon begins to weep, saying it has had enough.

Now it is earth's slave. The Iron Man asks the creature what it can do.

The dragon calls itself useless, saying all they do in space is fly or make music. It is a star spirit and sings the music of the spheres that makes space so peaceful.

The Iron Man asks why it tried to eat up the earth. It says it got excited by the war-cries of earth and wanted to join in.

The Iron Man says it can sing for them instead. The creature is to live on the moon and fly around the earth each night singing.

The Iron Man returns to his scrap-yard a hero. He receives many gifts to eat.

The space-bat-angel's singing has a wonderful effect on the world. It makes everybody peaceful and they live pleasantly alongside one another, enjoying the music from the giant singer in space.

Questions

1. How do they get the Iron Man to Australia?

2. What supplies has the Iron Man ordered?

3. What do the team of engineers do?

4. How does the Iron Man address the dragon?
   How does the dragon respond to this?

5. What challenge does the Iron Man have for the dragon?
   How does the dragon respond to this?
   What is your response?

6. What must the dragon do, if the Iron Man proves to be stronger than it?

7. Does the dragon seem worried to you?

8. Do you feel confident about this plan? Why/why not?

9. How is this conversation watched by the people of earth?

10. What makes the space-bat-angel-dragon agree to this challenge?

11. What have the engineers done with the girders?

12. What does the Iron Man do?

13. What effect does the heat have on the Iron Man?

14. Describe the Iron Man as he cools.

15. Is the monster afraid to lie on a bed of fire?

16. What will act as the monster's fiery bed?
    How does the monster feel about this?

17. What happens to the monster when it lands on the sun?

18. What happens when the creature lands on Australia?

19. Describe the creature after his spell on the sun.
    What effect does the heat have on the dragon?
    Do you feel sorry for the dragon here?

20. What is the Iron Man's next move?

21. How does the space-bat-angel-dragon react to this?
    How would you feel, in its position?

22. How is the Iron Man feeling, as he lies back in the flames?

23. Why does he grin at the dragon?

24. Are the engineers hopeful that the Iron Man will win?
    Why/why not?

25. What happens the moment the Iron Man begins to melt?
    Is he very lucky here, do you think?

26. How is the Iron Man feeling after his ordeal in the flames?

27. Does the monster mind having to return to the sun?
    Why does it go once more?
    Would you, in its position?

28. Describe the space creature's return flight to earth.

29. How does it land this time?

30. Describe the dragon's condition at this point.
    Do you feel sorry for the creature?

31. What does the Iron Man announce on the monster's return?

32. How does the space-bat-angel-dragon react?

33. "I feel like going on. We've only had two each."
    Do you believe the Iron Man's words here?
    What makes him say this?

34. What does losing mean for the space-bat-angel-dragon?

35. What music does the dragon make?

36. Why did the dragon want to eat up the earth?
    What is your response to this?

37. What task does the Iron Man set for the dragon?

38. Is the dragon being treated fairly by the Iron Man, do you think?

39. Why aren't people frightened of the space-bat-angel-dragon as it flies around earth each night?

40. What is its singing like?

41. How is the Iron Man being treated?

42. What is the effect of the dragon's music on the world? Are you surprised that this creature's music has this effect on the world?

43. Is this a happy ending?

Further Questions

1. Describe Hogarth, using examples from the text to support your ideas.

2. Describe the Iron Man, using examples from the text to support your ideas.

3. In what ways are Hogarth and the Iron Man similar? Refer to examples from the story in your answer.

4. Does the Iron Man treat the space-bat-angel-dragon fairly or unfairly?
   Use examples to support the points that you make.

5. Did the space-bat-angel-dragon expect to lose the challenge?
   Why/why not?

6. Does the Iron Man outsmart or deceive the space creature in this story?
   Use examples to support your point of view.

7. How do humans treat the Iron Man and the space-bat-angel-dragon in this story?
   Does this tell you anything about the attitude of humans towards what they do not know or understand?

8. What human qualities does the Iron Man have in this story?

9. What human qualities does the space-bat-angel-dragon have in this story?

10. What is the mood like as the story ends?
Can you explain what makes it this way?

11. Is there a moral to this story?
What could it be?

12. In what ways is this story a fairytale?
Does it remind you of any other stories you know?

13. How important are illustrations for a story like this?

14. What key illustrations would you choose to help tell this story?

15. Is the world of this story a violent place?

16. Why, in your opinion, did the author choose to tell this story?

17. What lesson does the author share with us in this novel?
Is this a valuable lesson, do you think?

18. Describe the time and place this story is set in (the world of the novel).
What is appealing about this time and place?
What is unappealing about it?
Include examples in your answer.

19. What are the main themes/issues in this novel?
    Explain your choices, using examples from the text.

20. Does this story teach us anything about technology or the natural world?

21. What do you like about this novel?
    Include examples in your answer.

22. What do you dislike about this novel?
    Include examples in your answer.

23. Who is your favourite character?
    What do you like and admire about them?

24. Which character do you dislike most?
    Explain what makes you dislike them.

25. What different elements of the story combine to make this novel exciting?

26. Do you like the ending?
    Does the ending complete the story?

27. Was there anything in the story that you would have liked to know more about?
    Explain your answer fully, including examples.

28. Would this story make a good film?
    What actors would you choose to play the key roles?
    Explain your choices.

29. What was your favourite part of this story?
    Why did this section appeal to you?

30. Does this novel remind you of any other novels, films or television programmes?
    Explain your choices.

31. What cover design would you choose for this novel?
    Give reasons for your answer.

32. Would you recommend this novel to a friend?
    Why/why not?

CLASSROOM QUESTIONS GUIDES

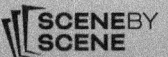

Books of questions, designed to save teachers time and lead to rewarding classroom experiences.

www.SceneBySceneGuides.com

www.ingramcontent.com/pod-product-compliance
Lightning Source LLC
Chambersburg PA
CBHW071507080526
44587CB00016B/2718